Bitcoin:

Beginner's Simplified Guide to Make Money with Bitcoin

Gavin S. Finney

various sources. Please consult a licensed professional before attempting any techniques outlined in this book.

By reading this document, the reader agrees that under no circumstances are is the author responsible for any losses, direct or indirect, which are incurred as a result of the use of information contained within this document, including, but not limited to, —errors, omissions, or inaccuracies.

Table of Contents

What This Book Will Teach You

Are you curious to learn about making money from Bitcoin but unsure where to start?

Have you always wanted to learn more about Bitcoin, but are intimidated by the technical jargon being used?

If these questions relate well with you, then this book is for you. In this book, you will find the basic essentials to learning about Bitcoin. This book introduces readers to the investing side of Bitcoin, the in's and out, the various processes and steps involved in it.

Who this Book is for

This book contains information on how to learn about Bitcoin from a beginner level.

Readers who can benefit the most from the book include:

- Individuals interested in making money from Bitcoin

- Investing enthusiasts who want to learn about Bitcoin as another possible source of income

- Readers who would like to know information about Bitcoin

How this Book is Organized

This book is organized into three parts. The parts are best read in chronological order. Once you become familiar with all the steps outlined in the book, you can go directly to the techniques which apply to your current situation the best.

The three parts of the book are:

Part One outlines the essential topics on Bitcoin. The section also talks about how important it is to learn these topics as a beginner in order to form a solid foundation in doing the right steps – from introductory concepts to making your first Bitcoin transaction.

Part Two is about the Investing and Trading side of Bitcoin and what investing mistakes you can avoid in order to help minimize the chances of you losing your money. You'll learn how the process works and how to implement the steps discussed.

Part Three are the other important topics on Bitcoin such as:

- Risk Management Essentials
- Bitcoin Mining Essentials

After each chapter, you will be provided with lessons and exercises in order to leverage the information found on this book.

By reading and implementing the steps outlined on this book, you will be able to understand Bitcoin essentials in helping you achieve your money-making goals.

Introduction:

I would like to thank you for purchasing this book, '*Bitcoin: Beginner's Simplified Guide to Make Money in Bitcoin.*'

Cryptocurrencies have been around for a while, and it is the collective term used for referring to digitized currencies that are encrypted cryptographically. The first cryptocurrency was invented in the year 2009, and it is known as the Bitcoin. These decentralized and digitized currencies have the power of changing the world of trade and commerce. All the systems of fiat currency that are in use at present need the involvement of a controlling authority for their production, management and control.

Instead, cryptocurrencies are formed on a peer-to-peer trading model, which eliminates the need of all intermediaries in their functioning. There are plenty of benefits that Bitcoins offer that goes beyond the ease of usage and efficiency.

In this book, you will learn the basics of Bitcoin, its history, benefits of using Bitcoins, about investing in Bitcoins and storing Bitcoins.

If you are interested in making the most of the digital revolution that has taken the world of finance and commerce by storm, then it is essential that you understand more about Bitcoins. So, let us get started now.

Chapter 1:

What is Bitcoin?

BITCOIN

Chapter 1: What is Bitcoin?

Background and definition

Bitcoin refers to a cryptocurrency that is created and is held in an electronic form. There is no regulatory authority or a centralized body that controls it, unlike all the other kinds of fiat currencies we use. Unlike fiat currencies, Bitcoins aren't printed, and they don't exist in a tangible form. A network of users who are spread all over the globe controls Bitcoins. The system makes use of a set of complicated mathematical equations along with an extensive web of computers for its functioning and maintenance.

The first cryptocurrency that was invented is the Bitcoin, and it was created by an anonymous entity- Satoshi Nakamoto. Just like any other form of fiat currency, even Bitcoins can be made use of for acquiring other commodities. However, an essential differentiating factor between Bitcoins and conventional money is that the former is decentralized. A decentralized network means that no central or regulatory authority is responsible for controlling the network. It also says that all the users of the system are the only ones who are in control of their funds instead of an intermediary.

Satoshi Nakamoto, an anonymous software developer, proposed the idea of Bitcoins when he published a white paper describing the working of a digitized currency functioning on a peer-to-peer network. Nakamoto's design was the creation of a form of money that doesn't need a central authority for its functioning and is capable of being transferred somewhat automatically and instantly. Since Bitcoins don't exist in a tangible form and are created digitally, they cannot be printed. Fiat currencies provide banks and other central regulatory authorities with the power of minting more money to cover any financial debts of the economy. Anyone is capable of joining the Bitcoin network.

Bitcoins are mined by using a well-distributed network of computers, and the system is responsible for the verification and processing of transactions. Therefore, Bitcoin manages to create a network of operations that is self-sufficient in its functioning. However, it doesn't mean that unlimited Bitcoins can be created. The Bitcoin protocol is designed in such a manner that it imposes a cap on the number of Bitcoins that can be created. The limit is set at 21 million, and once this limit is reached, the production of Bitcoins ceases altogether. A distinct feature of a Bitcoin is that it can be divided into several minor components. The smallest divisible element is referred to as Satoshi, after its creator, and it is equivalent to one hundred millionth of a single Bitcoin.

Why learn about Bitcoin

Bitcoin is quite a useful cryptocurrency, and all

the benefits it offers make it quite accessible. In this section, you will learn about the various benefits a Bitcoin provides to its users.

- Financial self-determinism: No one has the power to take Bitcoins away from the user without his or her consent. No regulatory authority can freeze your account or even stop you from transacting on the Bitcoin network. All credit cards operate on a pull mechanism. The minute you give the card to the vendor for payment, you are providing him access to your credit line. Once the vendor initiates the payment, the amount is automatically debited from your account, whereas with Bitcoins, the holder of Bitcoins needs to authorize a transaction and without the authorization, a deal will not be processed. Once you have your Bitcoins, no one can take these away from you, and no one has the power to freeze your Bitcoin account or prevent you from entering into any transactions on the

Bitcoin network. Whenever you use your credit card to make a payment, the vendor will have access to your credit line. A credit card usually uses a pull mechanism, and once the store/merchant has initiated the payment, then the amount will be automatically debited from your account, whereas Bitcoins make use of push technique. Unless the holder of Bitcoins authorizes a transaction, no one can debit your Bitcoins.

- Irreversible: Bitcoin transactions cannot be reversed intrinsically. Once a Bitcoin transaction is verified and is included in the blockchain, no one can modify it. The Bitcoin system operates on mutual trust, and once a payment is made, the same cannot be replaced without the approval of the vendor. So, it helps in solving the problem of chargebacks. Not just that, the Bitcoin network also helps to improve the security and the safety of a transaction.

- Elimination of intermediaries: Bitcoin is a peer-to-peer network. It means that there are no intermediaries like a bank or any other regulatory authority involved in a transaction. When there aren't any middlemen concerned, there won't be any transaction fees that need to be paid either. The only parties involved would be the sender and the receiver.

- Universal acceptance: Bitcoins can be transferred from one part of the world to another without any restrictions. You don't have to worry about territorial borders or even any bank holidays for transferring funds now. There aren't any artificial trading barriers, and it is quite easy to transact as well.

- Secure network: Merchants cannot charge any additional fees without attracting the attention of the buyer. They will need the prior permission of the other party as well. Also, no private information of either of the parties needs to be divulged to finalize a transaction. All this helps in securing personal information from potential threats of hacking. Bitcoin can be further encrypted to ensure the security of the users.

- Inflationary hedge: Only a finite number of Bitcoins can be in existence and once this limit is reached, production of Bitcoins ceases automatically. Also, this limit helps to provide the investor with a hedge against inflation.

It is important to learn the basics of Bitcoins because

- It would be foolish to invest your hard-earned money without understanding the basic workings of a particular form of investment. Would you want to invest in the stocks of a company that you know nothing about? Well, the same logic applies to Bitcoins as well.

- Understanding about Bitcoins will help

you to make an informed decision and also helps you to plan a strategy that works well for you.

- Learning and acquiring knowledge is the best way to move forward in today's world.

A Bitcoin transaction:

- It has been mentioned that Bitcoin is a peer-to-peer network. However, what does a peer-to-peer network mean? In this section, you will learn about how a basic Bitcoin transaction works. For instance, let us assume that A wants to send some Bitcoins to B. The transaction between A and B will be divided into three parts, and these are as follows.

- The first part is the input. The input contains the record of the address from which the sender (A) has received the Bitcoins. The second bit contains the amount. The amount refers to the quantum of Bitcoins that A is sending to

B. The third bit contains output, and it refers to B's wallet address.

- Two things are needed to send Bitcoins. The first one is the Bitcoin address and a private key to authorize the transaction. The Bitcoin address is a combination of letters and numbers that are randomly generated. The private key is also a sequence of letters and numbers, but unlike the address, this information is kept secret.

- The Bitcoin address is like a glass deposit box. Everyone knows what it contains, but only the person with the private key can access it.

- When 'A' wants to send Bitcoins to 'B,' then 'A' uses the private key to send a message with the input and the amount to 'B.'

- Once this is done, 'A' sends the Bitcoins to 'B.' Once a transaction takes place, the miners verify it, solve it, and the transaction becomes a part of the blockchain network.

CHAPTER SUMMARY:

In this chapter, you were familiarized with

- The basic history and meaning of a Bitcoin

- The different advantages a Bitcoin has over regular fiat currency we use, and

- The basics of a Bitcoin transaction.

YOUR QUICK START ACTION STEP:

Well, now that you know what a Bitcoin is and how it was created, the next step would be to learn a little more about its history and the reasons for which it was created. You can visit www.coindesk.com, to learn more about Bitcoins.

Chapter 2:
Why Bitcoin Can
Be
a Good
Investment

Chapter 2: Why Bitcoin Can Be a Good Investment

Investing in digital currency and Bitcoin

Cryptocurrencies, especially Bitcoin, are a great investment opportunity for all potential investors. An investment usually refers to an asset or an item that is acquired in the hope that it will generate a good income or return, and appreciate in future.

From an economic perspective, it refers to the purchase of goods that cannot be consumed immediately but leads to the creation of wealth in the future. From a financial perspective, investment relates to a monetary asset that is acquired with the idea that the asset will provide an income in the future or that it could be sold for a profit later on. When it comes to investment in Bitcoins, the definition of an investment doesn't change. Investing in Bitcoins is done with the aim that it could be sold for a profit later on.

It is a general belief that cryptocurrency is the future of the world of trade and finance. All the supporters of Bitcoins are of the opinion that it facilitates quicker and fuss-free transactions all over the world. Unlike fiat currencies, Bitcoins aren't backed by any governments or other centralized agencies, but they can be exchanged for any form of fiat currency like dollars, pounds, euros, and so on.

The fact that it can be immediately liquidated into any underlying type of money is the reason why investors are attracted to it. It is as good as holding gold in hand. As with any other monetary asset, the aim of investing in Bitcoins is to buy it at a low price and then sell it at a higher rate. The best way in which you can amass currency is by purchasing Bitcoins through an exchange and then selling them later on.

Bitcoin as an investment

Bitcoin is being viewed as a significant investment because of all the benefits it offers. Here are the main reasons why it is regarded as a brilliant investment.

- The inflationary risk associated with Bitcoins is quite low. Different governments control currencies all over the world. The main reason why the prices of currencies fluctuate is that states have the power to print more and more money. When there is an excess of money in circulation, the currency automatically loses its value, due to a reduction in its buying power. It essentially means that you will end up paying more money to acquire products. It is akin to a tax on all that is received, which in the end might not be sufficient. When it comes to Bitcoins, they are finite and therefore, you never have to worry about a reduction in its value. The forces of demand and supply govern the Bitcoin market. Since there cannot be an increase in amount with an increase in demand, the prices of Bitcoin will increase without any reduction in their value.

- When compared to all the other currencies, Bitcoin investors have a lower risk of failing. It is because of the simple fact that the production and trade of Bitcoins aren't dependent on the policies of governments. Governments might collapse, and the value of currencies might fall due to hyperinflation, but all this won't affect Bitcoins. Since a different protocol that is independent of the governmental policies controls the network, Bitcoin investors needn't worry.

- Apart from this, Bitcoin transactions are quite simple and easy to process. Buyers cannot try and reclaim their money after a purchase, and this gives the sellers a chance to ship their products or services to the buyer without worrying about any recoveries.

- You cannot carry vast sums of money around in your wallet, can you? Bitcoins are portable, so you needn't worry about that. Cash amounting to several million cannot be physically moved around without a lot of security. Therefore, Bitcoins are a better investment. With Bitcoins, you can carry around Bitcoins valued over several million in a simple memory card.

- Since Bitcoins aren't held with a third-party for safe-keeping, the holder has complete control over them. It means that you don't have to entrust the responsibility of safekeeping of your funds to anyone apart from yourself. Finally, Bitcoins cannot be traced. It means that the government has no possible way to discover the source of your funds!

Basic foundation about Bitcoin investment

There is no doubt that Bitcoins are the hottest

and the fastest growing of all digital currencies. There is no better time than the present to invest in Bitcoins. There are several success stories of investors who have amassed great wealth by investing in this form of cryptocurrency. To invest in Bitcoins, you need to follow the following steps.

- The first step is to select a Bitcoin wallet. A Bitcoin wallet is a virtual or an offline wallet that you will use to store and secure your Bitcoins. There are several wallets and types of wallets available for you to choose from. A couple of favorite Bitcoin wallets are Coinbase, Coindesk, and LocalBitcoins.
- Once you have a Bitcoin wallet, the next step is to check the current market value of the Bitcoin. Like any other form of currency, the amount of Bitcoin will not be constant. By observing the Bitcoin price movement for a while, you will get an idea about when you should jump into the game.

- The third step is the determination of the investment you are willing to make. Take into consideration all factors when you are figuring this out. Never invest more than you can stand to lose. Always invest in a positive attitude, but be prepared for the worst as well.
- The fourth and the final step is to buy Bitcoins. Different Bitcoin websites offer various forms of payments. Depending on a method of payment that meets your requirements, select a site.

CHAPTER SUMMARY:

In this chapter, you were introduced to the concept of Bitcoin investment.

- The meaning of Bitcoin investment is the same as that of any other investment. Bitcoin is a financial asset with high potential for growth and therefore is a brilliant investment.
- There are several reasons why someone would want to invest in Bitcoins. With

Bitcoins, the power of controlling the asset and its safekeeping rest in the hands of the investor. There isn't any governmental regulation. Therefore, the risk of inflation and devaluation are easily tackled. It is an excellent way to increase wealth and maintaining anonymity.

- There are a couple of simple steps that you should follow to invest in Bitcoins. You need to select a Bitcoin wallet, then check the Bitcoin market price, then determine the quantum of investment you are willing to make, and finally decide an ideal source of payment to acquire your investment.

YOUR QUICK START ACTION STEP:

The information provided in this chapter about Bitcoin investing isn't exhaustive. If you are interested in acquiring more knowledge about this topic, then you should head over to www.99Bitcoins.com! Spend some time and read about Bitcoin investments in great detail.

Chapter 3: How Bitcoin works

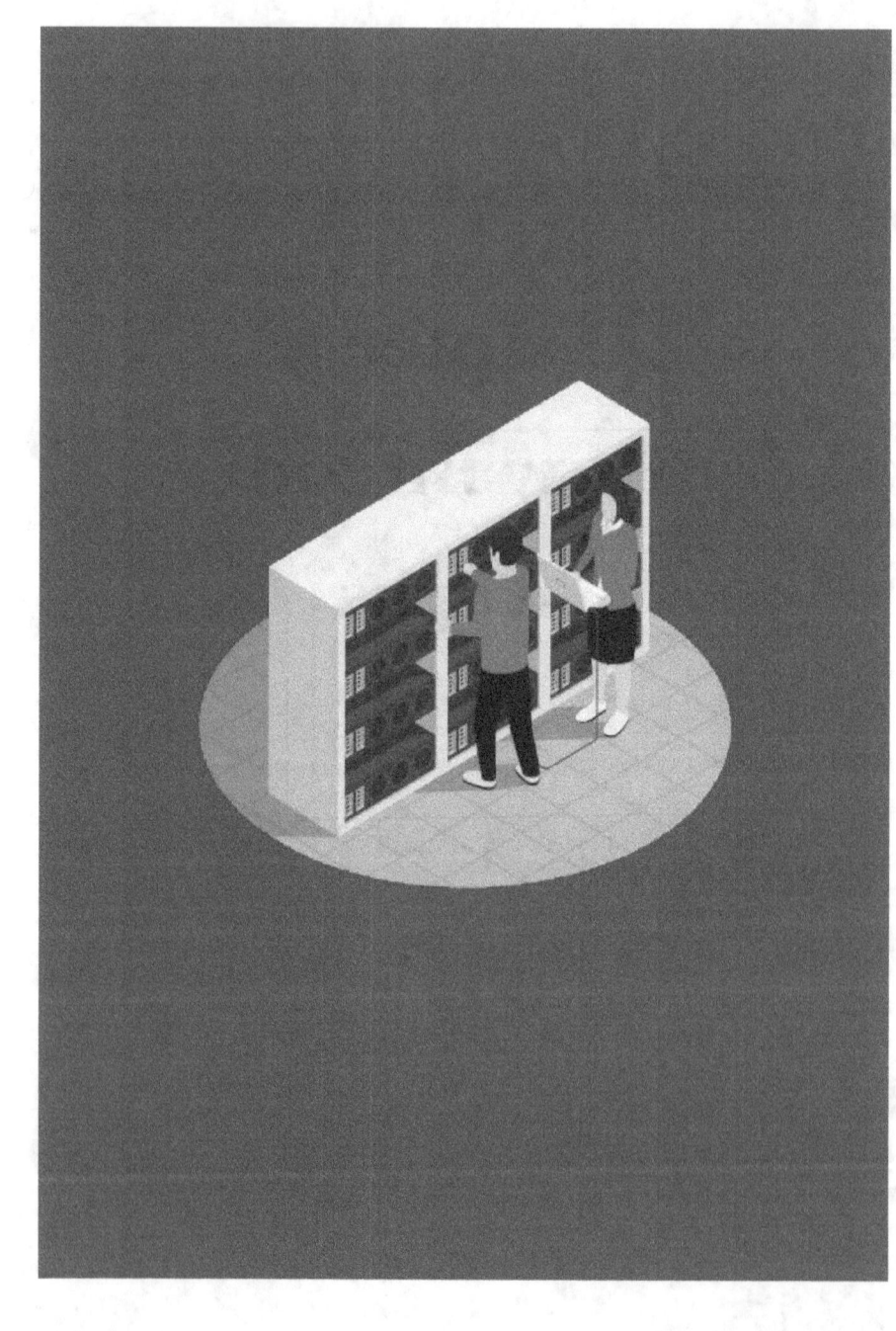

Chapter 3: How Bitcoin works

Fiat currencies and cryptocurrencies are fundamentally different. However, there are a couple of similarities between them. For instance, both forms of currencies can be made use of to acquire other things. Unlike dollars and pounds, any government or a legal tender doesn't back Bitcoins. Bitcoins are decentralized in nature and aren't linked to a central government or any other type of regulatory authority. It consists of a global system of users and computers and is based on different protocols of encryption and mathematical equations.

Bitcoins are used for conducting real transactions. For transacting, the first step is to acquire Bitcoins using your favored method of banking. Once you have acquired Bitcoins, they will be stored in your Bitcoin wallet for safekeeping. You can send or even receive payments from the vendor without the involvement of any intermediaries like banks or credit card companies. When intermediaries are eliminated, the transaction fees are reduced drastically. Every party to a transaction also enjoys a higher level of security and anonymity. A transaction in Bitcoins is quite similar to transacting with regular currency. Transactions conducted with Bitcoins cannot be traced.

Spending and receiving Bitcoins is almost as simple as sending an email, and you just need your computer or smartphone for this purpose. Several complex mathematical equations are utilized to ensure legitimacy and security of the transactions. There isn't a central computer that governs the network. Instead, all the computers used for transacting form a part of the Bitcoin network. These computers are responsible for generating and logging all the transactions that take place. The Bitcoin network is decentralized and is therefore resilient to the meddling of governmental agencies and regulatory authorities. Fiat currencies are printed, whereas Bitcoins are mined. So, they need to be mined before they enter the market. The mining of Bitcoins is similar to the production of currency notes, without a controlling authority. The application used for mining is available free of cost and it can be downloaded onto any computer for the sake of mining. The totality of all the users on the network along with their computers needs to complete a fixed amount of work before they get Bitcoins as a reward. The work is related to number crunching and the computer that cracks the code before the rest gets the reward. Some people have started investing in supercomputers to simplify the process of solving the mathematical equations. Not just that, miners tend to pool in their resources and form groups to solve blocks of the code. The precise amount of work that's cut out for them isn't fixed and is variable. Depending on the number of Bitcoins mined, the blockchain keeps tweaking the blockchain in a predetermined manner at a steady pace. It will keep doing this until all the 21 million Bitcoins have been mined. At present, about 25 Bitcoins are created every 10 minutes. The Bitcoin protocol is designed so that after every four years, the number of coins that can be mined will be reduced by half. Once the threshold has been reached, the number of coins in circulation will come to a standstill. Bitcoins are capable of being stored in a digital wallet. Whenever you are sending or receiving Bitcoins, a digital signature is used for their verification. The digital signature is referred to as the public encryption key. It helps in prevention of counterfeiting of transactions. Technically, you don't hold any Bitcoins in your wallet. Instead, all the public encryption keys validating the transactions you conducted are stored in it.

Why it is important to know how Bitcoin works

It is essential to know how a Bitcoin works if you are interested in acquiring any Bitcoins. Purchasing something without understanding its basics is a foolish decision and a rookie mistake. When you are capable of understanding how a Bitcoin works, you will be able to keep an eye on the way the transactions are taking place. You can become a vigilant investor. Not just that, you also be ready to start mining. You cannot mine for Bitcoins if you don't understand how Bitcoin mining takes place.

Basic framework of how Bitcoin works

As someone who is not aware of how Bitcoin works, you might not understand all the technical aspects involved in a Bitcoin transaction. After installing a Bitcoin wallet of your choice, it will help you to generate your Bitcoin address. After this, you can use it to create more addresses if need be. Your Bitcoin address is public information, and you can disclose it to anyone you want to.

Balances- blockchain

The blockchain is a public ledger, and the Bitcoin network is based on it. Once a transaction is confirmed, it forms a part of the blockchain. In this manner, the Bitcoin wallets will be able to calculate their available balance and, at the same time, new transactions can be verified rather easily. Cryptography helps to ensure the chronological order of the blockchain along with its integrity.

Transactions- private keys

A transaction on the Bitcoin network is in fact, a transfer of value between different Bitcoin wallets that forms a part of the blockchain. Bitcoin wallets store the private keys that are used for signing transactions and providing proof of ownership. The signature also helps to prevent the duplication of operations. Every purchase is broadcasted on the network, and the miners on the system verify its authenticity.

Processing- mining

Mining is the process that is used to confirm a transaction by including it on the blockchain. It helps in giving the blockchain a chronological order that is approved by all the nodes that form the Bitcoin network. Mining helps to generate Bitcoins as well.

CHAPTER SUMMARY:

In this chapter, you were provided information

about the primary working of a Bitcoin.

- The Bitcoin makes use of a digitized network of computers and users scattered all over the world to conduct and process transactions.
- It is essential to understand how a Bitcoin works for the sake of investing and mining.
- There are a couple of different segments that help a Bitcoin function. These sections are the blockchain, private keys, and mining.

YOUR QUICK START ACTION STEP:

If you are interested, you can visit www.investopedia.com for gathering more information about how a Bitcoin works.

Chapter 4:
The Bitcoin
Blockchain

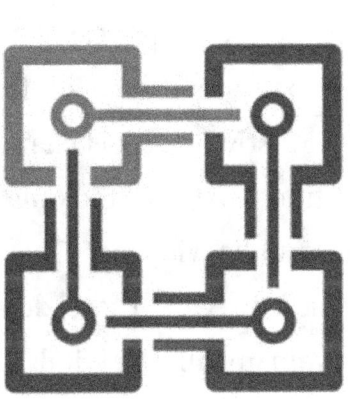

Blockchain

Chapter 4: The Bitcoin Blockchain

Background and definition of blockchain

The blockchain is a distributed database that keeps a list of ever-increasing record of transactions that are protected from editing and altering. Mostly, the blockchain is a ledger of all transactions that ever took place, and it is available for public viewing. The blockchain allows a person to view these details in real time, and evaluate all the vital stats of the system, like the time between each block, the number of blocks, cost of mining, fee per transaction, and even the electricity required for mining a single Bitcoin. With regards to Bitcoins, the blockchain is a digital ledger that is secured by cryptography, which prevents any tampering of the network. Usually, a blockchain is a network of computers. Whenever a new transaction takes place, it needs to be validated across the system before it becomes a part of the blockchain network.

The origin of the blockchain is nothing short of a fantastic thriller. It all started when an anonymous programmer by the name Satoshi Nakamoto published a detailed white paper. Satoshi provided a well-detailed outline of an innovative cryptocurrency that's based on a complicated mathematical formula and a robust network that's well distributed. Nakamoto's publication described how Bitcoins could be used for processing payments between two consenting entities without the involvement of a third party. Each transaction that takes place is recorded in the ledger of the blockchain and every block on it is linked to the previous one using a digital signature. To make the accounting trustworthy, the participants need to run it through several complicated algorithms to authenticate the signature before it can be a part of the blockchain. The ingenious blockchain technology allows total strangers to transact with each other in cyberspace. By 2014, there were more than 80 uses of such a technique.

The blockchain has been described as "*a programming language that allows users to write more sophisticated smart contracts, thus creating invoices that pay themselves when a shipment arrives or share certificates which automatically send their owners dividends if profits reach a certain level,*" by The Economist. The implementation of the blockchain consists of two types of records - block and blocks. Blocks record all transactions and every transaction carried out needs to be confirmed and cleared before it becomes a part of the public ledger. Not just that, every block contains a bit of the previous block. Thereby all the blocks are connected, and it forms an unbreakable chain. The authenticity of the blockchain is created because of this bond between the blocks on the network. All transactions are time stamped because of this innovative technique, and no one can change or alter a deal without changing the composition of the entire blockchain. There are two types of records that the blockchain implementation is made of, and these are blocks and blocks. In a block, the presence of a transaction confirms the sequence of the transaction along with its time. Users, who are known as miners, generate blocks and they make use of specialized mining software to verify the transactions present in each block, and the sequence so generated will form a part of the subsequent block.

Why understand the basics of blockchain

- It is essential to understand the basics of a blockchain because it is the technology that powers Bitcoins. Not just Bitcoins, most of the cryptocurrencies present in the market today make use of the blockchain technology. So, if you are thinking about investing in other cryptos, then it is quintessential that you understand about the functioning of the blockchain.
- Blockchain has several uses, and there is a good chance that it can, in fact, be absorbed into different aspects of

commerce all over the bank. Well, several major banks like JP Morgan and Goldman Sachs have joined a partnership for developing blockchain technology. By learning about blockchains, you are preparing yourself for future investments as well.

- Basic process of the blockchain
- The best and perhaps the most straightforward manner in which you can understand the Bitcoin blockchain is by thinking of it as a public transactional ledger. It helps in maintaining transparency of transactions on the network and helps to control the decentralized system of Bitcoins. The blockchain is responsible for recording, compiling, and verifying all the transactions that ever took place and are taking place at present. A web of users verifies every transaction and only after it is authenticated will it form a part of the blockchain. Since the Bitcoin network is decentralized, a single entity

can never change the entire data without alerting everyone on the web. The distribution of power and information make the system infallible while providing anonymity.

- The blockchain consists of large blocks of data that help in the verification and recording of all transactions. The network is aware of the movement of every coin and keeps track of all the coins generated. It is a public ledger with a record of transactions that took place in the past, are taking place at present, and all those transactions that will take place in the future as well. It is just like bookkeeping. When it comes to the functioning of an organization, accounting is vital. However, with Bitcoins, the record of transactions isn't private but public information. It doesn't mean that anonymity is lost because of it. The identity of the user is never disclosed. All that's available for public viewing are the wallet addresses.

The wallet address is just like your email address and mere access to the address doesn't make you vulnerable online. The identity of the holder or the owner of the address stays confidential while ensuring transparency of operations.

- The blockchain consists of different nodes. A node is a computer that's engaged on the network. So, all the machines of Bitcoin users used for transacting are nodes on the Bitcoin network. Any computer that is using a wallet application and is utilized for validating as well as detecting a transaction involving Bitcoins is a node. Every single node has access to the record of all the transactions. The blockchain keeps increasing whenever a new block of data is added to it. Every new block of data that is added contains the summary of the previous block, and therefore, the network cannot be altered. Up until 2013, more than 50 GB of data is stored on the blockchain.

- A block is always sealed by a miner, and all the miners compete with one another for mining. There is specific mining software that's used for this process. Whenever a miner generates the hash for a block, such miner will receive Bitcoins as a reward. The blockchain keeps updating itself regularly, and whenever it is updated, all the miners will get to know of it. The incentive of Bitcoins helps to maintain the miners engaging in the process, and it simultaneously assists in securing the network too. The hash of a block cannot be produced quickly, and the Bitcoin network is designed in such a way that with an increase in competition, the process of generating hash gets tricky. It makes use of a proof of work protocol.

- The protocol has been designed in such a manner that it doesn't reaccept an old hash and specific criteria need to be met. The hash of a block needs to be a specific sequence and should contain a predetermined number of zeroes. The tricky part is that there is no imaginable way in which a hash can be predicted before it has been created. As and when a new transaction is processed and added to the mix, the hash for the concerned block changes too. Miners on the network can view all the transactions, but they cannot tamper with any previous transactions. Instead, they should keep improving the manner in which the data is processed to produce the hash. They do this by using nonce, which is a random piece of data. The nonce is used in a transaction for creating its hash. If the hash doesn't fit into the given format, then the nonce has to be changed, and everything should be reformatted. It is seldom that someone finds the complete nonce in the first attempt. Miners keep trying until they find the perfect nonce. Whenever a miner obtains the correct hash, all the miners on blockchain will be informed of the same.

The Bitcoin network is a closed ecosystem that supports storage of data digitally.

CHAPTER SUMMARY:

- Bitcoins are powered by blockchain. The blockchain is an original technology that makes use of a web of computers and users located all over the world for the verification of transactions. Blockchain helps in maintaining the security and integrity of the network.
- It is essential to learn about blockchain if you are looking forward to investing in Bitcoins. If you wanted to spend in the stock of a company, you would want to learn about how it works, won't you? Well, the same principle of prudence applies to Bitcoin blockchain as well.
- Blockchain helps in the recording and the processing of transactions. It is in fact, a consolidation of all the Bitcoin

transactions that ever took place. Whenever a transaction takes place, miners verify the same across the world, and once it is validated, the blockchain is   updated.

YOUR QUICK START ACTION STEP:

The blockchain technology is ingenious and exciting. This futuristic technology can form the basis of several applications in the future and efforts are being made to discover various uses of it. In this chapter, you were introduced to the basic concept of a blockchain. You can visit www.techbullion.com to learn more about the blockchain technology.

Chapter 5: Making your first Bitcoin Transaction

Chapter 5: Making Your First Bitcoin Transaction

Different aspects of a Bitcoin transaction

Bitcoin was created with the intention of it functioning as a system of peer-to-peer electronic cash. Whether you are accepting or spending Bitcoin, it is wise that you understand how a Bitcoin transaction operates. Bitcoin transactions are quite similar to emails that are signed with digital signatures and are encrypted cryptographically before being sent to the Bitcoin network for verification. Transactional history is available for public viewing on the blockchain. Bitcoin is a chain of digitized signatures, and each holder can transfer Bitcoins to another by using a digital signature of the hash of the previous transaction and the Bitcoin address of the next. It is important to note that Bitcoins don't exist in your wallet, at least, not per se. All those Bitcoins in your wallet don't exist in the manner that cash or stock would. Bitcoins don't have a physical existence, and they aren't even stored on a server anywhere. The blockchain is the record of all transactions between Bitcoin addresses. These transactions are updated by the blockchain across all the nodes.

Steps for a Bitcoin purchase and its importance

A good Bitcoin wallet

Bitcoins are always stored in digital wallets. These wallets are used to hold Bitcoins while the holder decides to spend or exchange these coins. There are various wallets to choose from. The first step to buy Bitcoins is to get yourself a wallet to store your Bitcoins. In the world of cryptos, a wallet is used for storing your Bitcoins that are quite valuable. These wallets are similar to any of the bank accounts that you might use. Some are like regular spending accounts that are similar to a regular wallet that you carry with you and then there are others that have got a high level of security. Some can be used as daily spending accounts and then there are some that offer military-grade security. The main options that you have are a software wallet, an online or web-based wallet, and an offline vault or a multisig wallet that uses different keys to protect the account. All the wallets have certain advantages as well as disadvantages. You will learn more about the various wallets in the coming chapters. All those who have just started using Bitcoins might feel overwhelmed by the number of wallets and exchanges that they can choose from. Well, read on to learn more.

Bitcoin exchanges

There are several Bitcoin exchanges to choose from. There are proper exchanges for all the institutional traders, and then there are regular wallet services for those who are just interested in testing the waters. Most of the trading platforms have the provision to store or hold your fiat as well as digital currencies. Exchanges are great for not just trading in cryptocurrencies, but for saving them as well.

One-on-one meeting

You can meet the local Bitcoin users and decide if you want to buy or sell your Bitcoins. Various websites let you transact by facilitating individual sessions. For instance, LocalBitcoins allow the local Bitcoin buyers and sellers to meet. You can meet the other party that's interested in making the trade, and then you can decide for yourself if you want to finalize the deal or not.

Bitcoin mining

Another method that you can make use of to acquire Bitcoins is by mining for these coins. In order to mine, you will need a PC and powerful graphics card. ASICs are devices that are used explicitly for mining. The number of Bitcoins that are available will dwindle down slowly. Mining requires patience and investment. It means that mining isn't as cost-effective as it was a year ago. Most people end up spending more on the hardware and electricity than they could ever earn from mining. Mining is usually done in pools these days. It means a couple of miners will get together and pool in their resources for mining Bitcoins and then divide the rewards according to a predetermined ratio.

Bitcoin ATMs

It is a new concept, and it is slowly picking up speed. It is quite similar to a face-to-face exchange, but it involves a machine. You will have to insert your currency or scan the QR code of your wallet, and you will receive the necessary systems to load Bitcoins into your Bitcoin wallet. Exchange rates can vary, and it can be anywhere between 3-8%. Buying Bitcoins might not seem like an easy thing to do, especially for newcomers. However, the number of avenues available to buy these Bitcoins from is increasing.

CHAPTER SUMMARY:

There are different ways in which you can buy Bitcoins. You can buy Bitcoins by making use of an online wallet, an exchange service, a Bitcoin ATM, or even by facilitating a face-to-face meeting.

YOUR QUICK START ACTION STEP:

Well, now that you know how simple it is to buy Bitcoins, why don't you get started? Visit www.coindesk.com and www.coinbase.com to learn more about setting up a Bitcoin wallet and buying Bitcoins online.

Chapter 6:

Storing Bitcoins

Chapter 6: Storing Bitcoins

Methods of storing Bitcoins

An exchange

The easiest and the most straightforward manner would be to store the Bitcoins on an exchange. There are different exchanges to choose from, and you can select one of those. The simplest method isn't always the safest method. When you are storing your Bitcoins on an exchange, you don't have full control over it. Trading platforms are capable of being hacked, or they might even shut their operations without any prior notice. So, make sure that you are prudent while selecting an exchange.

Online wallet

There are several online wallets that you can make use of to store your funds, and these are better than the exchanges. A couple of online wallets that you can choose from are Coinbase, Coindesk, Circle, Coinkite, and Xapo. The benefit of using an online wallet for storing your Bitcoins is that you will have full control over your coins. You will be the only one who has the private keys. However, on the downside, the private keys are also stored online, and this makes them vulnerable to hacking. If your priority is ease of access and convenience, and security is secondary, then in such a case you should consider using an online wallet for storing your Bitcoins.

1. Coinbase: This is an excellent wallet, and it serves about 2.8 million countries and has spread its operations in over 32 countries with a turnover in Bitcoin exchange amounting to $2.5 billion. This wallet will directly link your bank account to the cryptocurrency exchange for converting cryptocurrency into fiat currency and vice versa. It has a mobile application that's developed for Android and iOS platforms as well as a web browser. All the cryptocurrency that is held within their servers are insured and even they offer a multi-signature vault for ensuring the

security of the cryptocurrency that lies within it.

2. Xapo: This is a simple wallet to use, and it allows the user access to the storage vault within which cryptocurrency is stored. It is based in Hong Kong, and this company offers cold storage for your funds that are encrypted and are locked behind walls made of concrete, steel doors, and cages that can block radio waves. What's more? They offer their debit card!

3. Coinkite: This is an innovative platform that allows its users to transfer Bitcoins via SMS, thereby making transactions much simpler and more accessible. Coinkite is a multi-signature wallet. It means that for every sale that needs to be approved, a combination of multiple keys is necessary for authentication. To put it just, if at all someone wants to hack your wallet, they will need a set of correct codes that need to be entered at the same time. Thereby

making it difficult to steal funds from your wallet.

Desktop wallet

When compared to the previous two options, storing your Bitcoins in a desktop wallet is a better idea. The good thing about desktop wallets is that only the private keys are stored on the local machine. Since the Personal keys are stored on your desktop, their exposure to threat and hacking is reduced significantly. However, it isn't a foolproof method. If a malware that can steal Bitcoins infects your computer, then you will be in trouble. Once you lose your coins, there is no possible manner in which you can acquire them again. Depending on the kind of desktop wallet you are using and the way in which you are setting it up, you can start transacting in Bitcoins anonymously. Your email and IP addresses won't be linked to your Bitcoin wallet.

Mobile wallet

Another secure manner in which you can store your Bitcoins is by storing them in a mobile wallet. Mycelium and Breadwallet are useful applications that can be downloaded onto your phone from the app store. The wallets can be set up without divulging any private information. So, you can make sure that the transactions will be confidential and anonymous. If you are making use of a burner phone for conducting your operations, then your phone ID or IMEI cannot be linked either. All the applications back up your data to your preferred location. With a mobile wallet, your private keys are stored on the mobile phone, and in case it is lost, you can always make use of the backup information for retrieving your coins.

Hardware wallet

If security were your priority, then one of the best forms of storing your Bitcoins would be in a hardware wallet. Trezor, KeepKey, and Ledger are a couple of examples of hardware wallets. Hardware wallets are a great way in which you can increase the security of all your funds stored in it. Also, this option of storage provides an entirely anonymous way of transacting in cryptocurrencies. No personal information is linked to the device and therefore, there is no scope for a breach of identity or data. The reason why hardware wallets are a good idea is that your private keys are always stored on a separate hardware device. Even if your computer gets attacked by a malware, it is impossible for it to get through to your hardware wallet. You can recover your funds quite quickly with the help of a seed phrase.

Paper wallet

When compared to other forms of wallets, paper wallets aren't all that popular. You need to have a better understanding of the protocol for using this type of wallets. You can generate a Bitcoin paper wallet from your online wallet option. You can even make it offline if you want to ensure more security. You just have to disconnect your computer from the Internet when you are creating your paper wallet. These wallets can be stored anywhere and don't take up any space. Not just that, they are the most anonymous manner in which you can save

Bitcoins. You have to make a note of your Bitcoin seed on a piece of paper, and that's about it. You can further secure this section by making copies of it and placing it in a couple of secure locations. It would be quite impossible for a hacker to steal some information that hasn't even touched the Internet.

Multisig wallets

Multi-signature wallets are also known as multisig wallets, and this method of storing Bitcoins is slowly gaining popularity. In this form of a wallet, the authorization of a person is required multiple times before a transaction can be processed. It is an excellent solution for all those who want to store their Bitcoins together. If you were pooling in your Bitcoins with someone else, then the wallet option that you should opt for would be this. For instance, let us assume that you don't want a single person to have the control of all your company's funds. Then in such a case, you set up multi-signature wallet wherein multiple executives would need to authorize a transaction before it can be transacted.

Burying the Bitcoins

Now that we are done with the most common storage options for your Bitcoins let us move on to the less obvious ones. If you are extremely concerned about the security of your Bitcoins and are worried that someone might gain access to your system or even rob your house, then in such a case, you can make a copy of your paper or hardware wallet, and bury your Bitcoins in your backyard! For additional security, you can make a backup of the buried wallet in the form of a paper wallet in case you forget the spot you buried it in.

Storing them in a bank

It might sound like the worst possible idea ever, but you can save your Bitcoins in a bank. It isn't all that bad. You have first to generate a paper wallet and then make a copy of the same and place this copy in your locker in the bank. The safety deposit boxes in the bank are quite secure, and they have 24*7 security. This method of storage guarantees anonymity and safety from physical hazards.

Benefits of using a Bitcoin wallet

- A Bitcoin wallet provides convenience. You can transact easily and quickly by utilizing a wallet.

- Not just convenience, it provides safety for your Bitcoins as well. Bitcoins are digitized currencies, and therefore, the threat of hacking and theft never goes away. You should take all the necessary precautions.

- You are the only one that's responsible for the safety of your tokens. So, you need to safeguard your coins against the threat from third parties as well as the risk you pose towards them.

CHAPTER SUMMARY:

- There are different types of wallets to choose from. Depending on your needs and requirements you can select any of the wallets that have been mentioned in this chapter.

- There are online and offline wallets. Depending on the ease of access and the level of security they offer, you should select one of the two types of wallets.

- Always make use of two wallets. One for storing your cryptos and the other for transacting.

- Once you lose the Bitcoins, there is no possible manner in which you can recover them. Not just that, it is essential to store your private key securely. You cannot restore your private key once you lose it.

YOUR QUICK START ACTION STEP:

Take some time out of your schedule and research more about the different wallets and how the work. Not just that; read about various precautions that you can take for safeguarding your investment.

Chapter 7: Investing in Bitcoin

Chapter 7: Investing in Bitcoin

There is no time like the present when it comes to starting something new. The first step while investing is to create an account for yourself with a site like Coinbase, Kraken, or anything else that you are comfortable with for converting your funds into cryptocurrencies. You can link up your credit or debit cards, or even your bank account with any such platform to facilitate the transfer of money. There are pros and cons of every platform that exists so you should always do plenty of research before trusting a platform. Now that you have made up your mind about the type of cryptocurrency you feel like investing in, then select a platform that is best suited for it.

The number of options that are available in the market these days is quite overwhelming. At least for the first few investments, make it a point to invest in cryptocurrencies that are quite popular. Like Bitcoin, Ethereum, Litecoin, dash, or ripple. It all depends on the kind of cryptocurrency you want to invest in. Bitcoin is considered to be the gold standard in the world of cryptocurrencies. Most of the cryptocurrencies make use of similar technology for their functioning. Don't opt for any obscure cryptocurrencies, especially when you are making your first purchase. Don't dive headfirst into the world of cryptocurrency investing. Instead, take small steps and get a feel for what you are investing in. Understand the market and the instruments involved. Don't spend all your money in one go.

Once you have figured out the crypto that you want to invest in, the next step is to find an ideal wallet for storing the same. Refer to the previous chapter for more information on crypto wallets. Select a wallet that will meet all your requirements.

You can never have too much knowledge about something. Keep researching and learning about all the new developments that keep taking place in the world of cryptocurrencies. If you have decided to invest in a particular cryptocurrency, then make it a point to make sure that you know all the recent changes taking place in it. Refer to different websites and magazines. Read the newspaper to track any last changes in that particular cryptocurrency and the way in which it would influence your investment.

There are plenty of social media platforms and blogs that you can refer to. Not just that, you can join different communities dedicated to various cryptocurrencies for making sure that you are learning about crypto and allied topics.

Basic investing principles

- Everywhere you look, you have got ideas, opinions and analysis available about investing. It is everywhere, on the television, Internet, magazines, newspapers and so on. You cannot get away from it. A successful investor might incorporate other's analysis into their analysis before making a decision.

However, the final decision is always based on their research.

- There are plenty of cryptocurrencies out there for you to invest in. Lots of them would have the potential for a good investment. However, this doesn't mean that you should invest in them. Invest in a cryptocurrency only when you understand how it functions. If you don't, then you are setting yourself up for failure. No, you don't have to know all the technical aspects of it; you just need to have an idea about how it functions.

- Having a diversified portfolio is essential. It helps to spread the risk. However, too much diversification is a bad thing. It causes the investor to be spread out too thin. A successful investor would have a diverse portfolio so that their risk is distributed optimally, but will ensure that it isn't so different that their resources are spread too thin.

- Media plays an active role in promoting investments these days. Invest in crypto that is well established and has a good team of developers. Learn more about them as well.

- If you don't have well-defined goals, then you cannot achieve anything in your life. How will you reach your goals without a well thought out strategy? Luck doesn't play a part when it comes to investing, and it indeed doesn't happen overnight. You will need a good investment strategy. To do that, you will need to determine a few things. Take into consideration your aptitude for bearing risk, the funds you will need, the kind of stocks you want to invest in, the portion of your income you would like to spend, and your exit strategy in case the market crashes.

Benefits of investing in Bitcoins

- Initially, when Bitcoins were introduced, they were meant to be used as digital currency for transacting over the Internet with minimal transactional fees. Since its inception, several uses of Bitcoin have been discovered. Bitcoins can be traded digitally; they can be used for acquiring other things, for settling insurance claims, paying remittances, and so on. Initially, it was quite challenging to find a vendor who would accept payment in the form of Bitcoins. However, with the increase in their popularity, this situation has been rectified. There are several online and offline merchants as well as vendors who have started accepting cryptocurrencies as a form of payments. Several of the big online retailers like Overstock, Newegg to small businesses, and restaurants are also taking cryptos. You can make use of Bitcoins for paying your bills, for shopping, and for acquiring goods as well. Apple has recently authorized that users can start purchasing their app store by making use of different cryptos. There are a couple of online marketplaces like OpenBazaar and Bitify that only accept cryptocurrencies as a form of payment.

- The potential of earning a profit is more than incurring a loss while you are investing in Bitcoins. The prices of Bitcoins have been steadily increasing, and it doesn't seem like it will decrease anytime soon. In 2017, the cost of a single Bitcoin is more than an ounce of gold!

Investing in Bitcoins

Wallets

The first thing that you will need to do would be to get yourself a wallet for your Bitcoins. After this, you will require a place for storing your Bitcoins. In the world of cryptocurrencies, a wallet is made use of for storing your Bitcoins. These wallets are quite similar to a bank account that you might have. Depending on the level of security that you are looking for, different wallets are available. Some are like regular spending accounts that are similar to a regular wallet that you carry with you and then there are others that have got a high level of security. Three different options are available to you. The first one is a software wallet that can be stored on the hard drive on your computer. The second option is to opt for an online service, and the third option would be to make use of a storage "vault" that would make use of private keys for protecting your account. Most of the wallets have their vulnerabilities. Always make sure that you store your Bitcoins locally on your computer and back up your wallet regularly so that even if the hard drive gets corrupted, you will still be able to access your account. When it comes to online wallets, make sure that you take all the necessary precautions for securing your Bitcoin account from hackers.

Bitcoin exchanges

There are plenty of Bitcoin exchanges as well as wallets to choose from. There are proper exchanges for institutional traders, and then there are wallet services that are available for someone who is just testing the waters. Most of the transactions, as well as wallets, will store the digital or fiat currency you hold, just like a traditional bank account would. Exchanges and wallets are an excellent option if you ever want to engage in trading. You don't need complete anonymity, and you don't have to take any extensive measures or go through any lengthy procedures that would require the disclosure of contact information and proof of identity. It is pretty much the law regarding trading of Bitcoins in most of the countries, and there is no way in which exchange can get around this system. These rules are quite similar to the ones that apply to any company that would be interacting with the financial system would require them to follow the KYC (know your customer) and AML (Anti-money laundering) guidelines.

The best exchange option that is available to you would depend on your location. At present, the most significant Bitcoin trading exchanges regarding volume are Bitfinex based in Hong Kong, Bitstamp in the US, BTC-e, Kraken based in the US, Huobi in China and Hong Kong, OKCoin and BTCC based in China. A famous exchange and wallet service that would allow for trading regarding US dollars as well as Euros are Coinbase. This company has a website and its mobile application as well. It was initially providing these services only in the US, but it has now expanded its operations to European countries as well. Circle offers its users across the world a chance for storing, sending, receiving, and exchanging Bitcoins. At present, only the citizens of US can link their bank accounts for depositing funds, but credit and debit cards are an option as well. There are mobile applications for iOS and Android platforms. Coinjar is an exchange that is located in Australia and provides the same services as the other platforms.

Once you have managed to set up your account, you will need to link your bank account and then make the necessary arrangements for moving these funds between them. People in most of the countries are allowed to transfer money to other accounts across different continents. However, the fee is on the higher side, and there could be some delays when you convert your Bitcoins into regular currency. If you have to link your bank account for using the exchange, then it might allow only the banks are belonging to that country.

One-on-one meeting

If you live in a big city, you like anonymity, and you don't want to get into the hassles of the banking system, then in such a case, you buy Bitcoins from a local seller. Different websites will allow for such transactions like LocalBitcoins. These sites will allow you to meet up with varying traders of Bitcoins and you can decide whether you want to finalize the trade or not. Remember, if you are meeting someone in person, then you will need to have instant access to your Bitcoin wallet and a good Internet connection for cinching the deal. There are a couple of security considerations that buyers and sellers should take while engaging in such trade. Meet in a public place, and don't go around carrying vast amounts of cash. If the concept of a one-on-one meeting doesn't appeal to you, then in such a case you can search for MeetUp groups as well.

Mining Bitcoins

The next method by which you can own Bitcoins would be by mining them. You need a PC and a powerful graphics card to get started with mining your Bitcoins. Specific mining devices are referred to as ASICs. The number of Bitcoins still available is steadily dwindling down as time progresses. It means that mining isn't as cost-effective as it was a year ago. Most people end up spending more on the hardware and electricity than what they could ever earn from mining. Mining is usually done in pools these days. It means a couple of miners would get together and pool in their resources for mining Bitcoins and then divide the rewards according to a predetermined ratio. This isn't for hobbyists.

Investment trust

If you aren't too comfortable with the idea of having to buy and then safely store large numbers of Bitcoins, then there is the option of an investment trust like Bitcoin Investment Trust or BIT. The trust will invest in Bitcoins, and it will make use of the specialized protocol for storing these Bitcoins on behalf of its shareholders. This is quite similar to how a mutual fund would function.

CHAPTER SUMMARY:

- In this chapter, you were provided with information about
- Investing in Bitcoins along with a couple of simple investing principles.
- The benefits of investing in Bitcoins.
- The different ways in which you can invest in Bitcoins.

YOUR QUICK START ACTION STEP:

The best way in which you can learn more about investing in Bitcoins is by actually investing in the market. Take some time out, device a strategy and start investing. Start with a small amount and depending on how your investment performs, you can spend more.

Chapter 8:
How to Avoid
Investing
Mistakes in
Bitcoin

Chapter 8: How to Avoid Investing Mistakes in Bitcoin

Common mistakes and how to avoid them

Keeping separate wallets

If you are making use of one wallet for spending your Bitcoins as well as your entire Bitcoin holdings, you will be making yourself a soft target. There isn't a limit on the number of addresses for Bitcoin wallets that a person can have. Therefore, you can make sure that you have a separate address for spending your money, for savings, and for the receipt of payments.

Your web wallet shouldn't have your savings

Web wallets are quite secure; however, they can be hacked into. If your web wallet can be hacked and it has all your savings, then you can just forget about your Bitcoins. Web wallets are quite convenient when it comes to usage, but you should just make use of them like you would use a current or a checking account. It is a place for holding a small amount of money that you would use in the foreseeable future. Therefore, if you just maintain a little balance in this wallet, even if the wallet gets hacked, the damage you suffer can be limited. Bitcoins sure don't work like a regular credit card. Even if you lose your money due to fraudulent activity, that money is gone, and there is no way in which you can get it back. You certainly cannot claim anybody. You could contact the police, but it is highly unlikely that they will be able to trace anyone.

Protecting your privacy

You are responsible for your security. Don't share any private keys with anyone. Think of your wallet address as your bank account and continuing the same analogy, your private key is like the PIN of your account. If you have got a spending and savings wallet, then the regular transactions that take place between these two will help in providing the hackers with a signal about which one is the savings wallet. Keeping all the illegal activities aside, would you want to divulge all your financial information to a complete stranger? Well, you certainly wouldn't want to. You should make use of a mixing service for the transfer of funds between these two wallets.

Cold storage

Even if you store your Bitcoins in a wallet that is stored on your computer, you will still be vulnerable. Applications of various Bitcoin wallets tend to save the user data in a particular location that can be easily predicted and this will make your financial information susceptible to an attack from any virus that can steal your data. Trojan horse attacks are the most commonly reported ones. A simple solution would be to keep the private key of your wallet on an offline medium. This will provide a little more security. An offline medium could be a QR code that is printed on a paper or a text file or a document stored on a USB. If you are looking for a way to transfer the Bitcoins you have in your offline wallet to someone or some other place, you should scan this QR code or enter the private key into the blockchain application. Once the balance in your wallet is displayed on the app, you can start transferring your Bitcoins to any address that you want to. You can get your private keys encrypted. This would render the key useless even if they get discovered since it would be worthless without the encryption password. However, make sure that you don't forget the password.

Backup

The previous tips have been about protecting your Bitcoins from others; this is about protecting your Bitcoins from yourself. If you are making use of your PC or your laptop, you will need a backup option for your wallet. These instructions would change depending on the client. The public and the private key of your wallet can be saved into a file. That's is all that a Bitcoin would need to retrieve your balance. Once the data containing your wallet keys is with you, you can pretty much store it anywhere you want to like a flash drive, optical disk, and so on. These files can also be stored on a cloud-based storage system like Dropbox.

Never invest more than you can afford to lose

There is some uncertainty that would accompany any time of investment. When it comes to an instrument like Bitcoin that is highly volatile and speculative, the chances of earning a profit are high, and on the downside, the loss you can incur is quite high as well. Poor decision-making can lead to massive losses when it comes to trading in Bitcoins. The investment that you make should be something that you are comfortable with. Prepare yourself for the worst outcome; you lose out on everything you invested. A successful investor would always want to diversify their portfolio. It is not wise to allocate all your funds towards a single class of asset because it increases your level of risk. If you invest more than what you can afford to lose, then in such a case your ability to make right decisions will be indeed impaired. There is something known as "panic selling." Don't indulge in this. There are bound to be inevitable ups and downs in the market conditions. Don't panic and sell your investment for a low price in a bid to cut your losses. This could just increase the loss that you have incurred.

Setting goals for every trade

It is incredibly vital to set goals. This helps in keeping your calm even during extremely volatile market conditions. More so in the case of Bitcoins. Before you place a trade, you should decide on the price at which you should take your profits and cut your losses and quit the game. You should determine this well in advance. It will help to prevent you from taking any emotional decisions that might or might not produce good results. A trader without a target price might have managed to make a profitable trade and then in his greed to earn more, might end up losing out on what he had as well. Having a plan will help you in staying levelheaded and rational during the highs and lows of the market.

CHAPTER SUMMARY

In this chapter, you were introduced to the concept of different mistakes that people tend to make while investing and the manner in which you can avoid all these mistakes. A little bit of prudence and patience are necessary for becoming a successful investor. Make sure that you aren't rushing in or out of a trade. Don't be emotional while making a deal and be practical. Never panic and sell your Bitcoins. Holding onto them is a better idea than getting rid of them.

YOUR QUICK START ACTION STEP:

Make a conscious note of the different points mentioned in this chapter for becoming a better investor. Keep these points in mind while you are making your next investment, and you will be able to see a positive change.

Chapter 9: Risk Management Essentials for Bitcoin Investing

Chapter 9: Risk Management Essentials for Bitcoin Investing

Risks and risk minimization

Investing is risky in general and investing in cryptocurrencies is a high-risk, high return activity. At present, there is no other category of investment that has potential as high as the one offered by cryptocurrencies. However, with high rewards, the risk involved is quite high too. As a crypto investor, there are a couple of chances that you should be aware of.

Cryptocurrencies and all kinds of digital tokens are considered to be extremely volatile. The volatility of Bitcoins has relatively reduced over the years, but all the other forms of cryptocurrencies experience intra-day price movements that can move in either of the directions. The market for cryptocurrencies is news-driven, and every crypto has its risk, rumors, sensationalized headlines, and spiteful media campaigns by the rival blockchain technologies can result in significant price drops and unfavorable fluctuations in the value of the cryptocurrencies. As an investor, you can significantly reduce your market risk by diversifying your investment portfolio. Your portfolio of cryptocurrencies shouldn't consist of just one form of crypto and should have smallholdings of other altcoins as well. You can further reduce your market risk by hedging your investment portfolio with BTC futures as well.

Another challenge that investors who are investing in mid-cap and small-cap coins are the risk of liquidity. At present, the average trading volume of Bitcoin per day is over $2 billion. If you leave the ten largest cryptos according to their market share, investors are left with a trading volume that's less than $100 million daily, and in most of the cases, it is less than $10 million. Anyone who is looking to make a more significant investment will find this situation quite challenging. Not just that, the trading volumes of the cryptos are spread over different exchanges, and it makes it quite tricky to execute a large order. For mitigating the risk posed by liquidity, try sticking to those cryptos that are quite liquid, especially when you are trading in large volumes.

Cryptocurrencies are a decentralized form of currencies. However, regulatory uncertainty poses to be a significant hurdle for any seller. Whenever a considerable cryptocurrency trading platform announces any adverse cryptocurrency norms, the entire market gets shaken. For instance, China had recently proclaimed a ban on ICOs (initial coin offerings), and this caused a significant drop in the prices of Chinese digital currencies like NEO. Regulatory risk isn't just confined to one region of the world. All those who invest in cryptocurrencies should follow any legal news about the tokens they are investing in quite regularly. At present, the major governments of the world haven't banned the use of cryptocurrencies. However, if they do so, then the effect can be devastating. Sadly, regulatory risk cannot be mitigated, and all that an investor can do is follow the news closely and act accordingly.

When it comes to trading cryptocurrencies and storing funds, operational risks are bound to exist. The major centralized Bitcoin exchanges happen to be frequent targets for cybercriminals. Even if you are making use of own wallets for storing your funds, you might still suffer a loss if you don't store your holdings in cold storage. If you are interested in minimizing the operational risk you face, then you should make use of decentralized exchanges and opt for hardware wallets while storing your funds.

Regardless of what you would like to believe, if you are investing in cryptocurrencies, you are a target for hackers. Most of the digitized currencies are pseudonymous, and this makes them an ideal target for cybercriminals out there. Unfortunately, the crypto space is filled with fake websites, fraudulent email campaigns, and targeted hacking of vulnerable trading platforms. A significant risk that crypto investors should be varied of is cybercrime.

There are no generalized tips for mitigating this risk, and as an investor, you should take all the necessary steps for ensuring the cyber-safety of your investments and holdings.

Numerous schemes promise unrealistically high returns and are often promoted across different social media platforms and at times are even advertised on reputable cryptocurrency media outlets. Usually, these are just pyramid schemes. However, scammers keep coming up with fraudulent ICOs for scamming novice investors. Prudence and research can prevent you from falling prey to such scams. Make sure that you are doing your research and aren't investing because someone asked or told you to.

Well, it might seem like there are plenty of risks that you might have to face as an investor, but you can successfully mitigate your chances by taking a couple of simple steps. Make sure that you keep these risks in mind before entering the cryptocurrency market.

CHAPTER SUMMARY:

Bitcoin is a significant investment indeed. However, certain risks are associated with any form of investment, and the same applies to Bitcoins as well.

- It is essential to understand the different risks you might face because it will help with better decision-making.
- When you are aware of all the risks you face as an investor, you can decide on the capital for investment. Not just that, you can come up with plans for preventing or avoiding such risks. If the risk isn't avoidable, you can take the necessary steps for reducing the damage such a risk might to.

YOUR QUICK START ACTION STEP:
As a potential investor, the first step of risk management that you should implement today is to understand the Bitcoin thoroughly. Learn as much as you can about it and keep learning. Follow different websites and chat groups to check for any latest developments regarding Bitcoins.

Bonus Chapter: Bitcoin Mining Essentials: The Benefits and How It Works

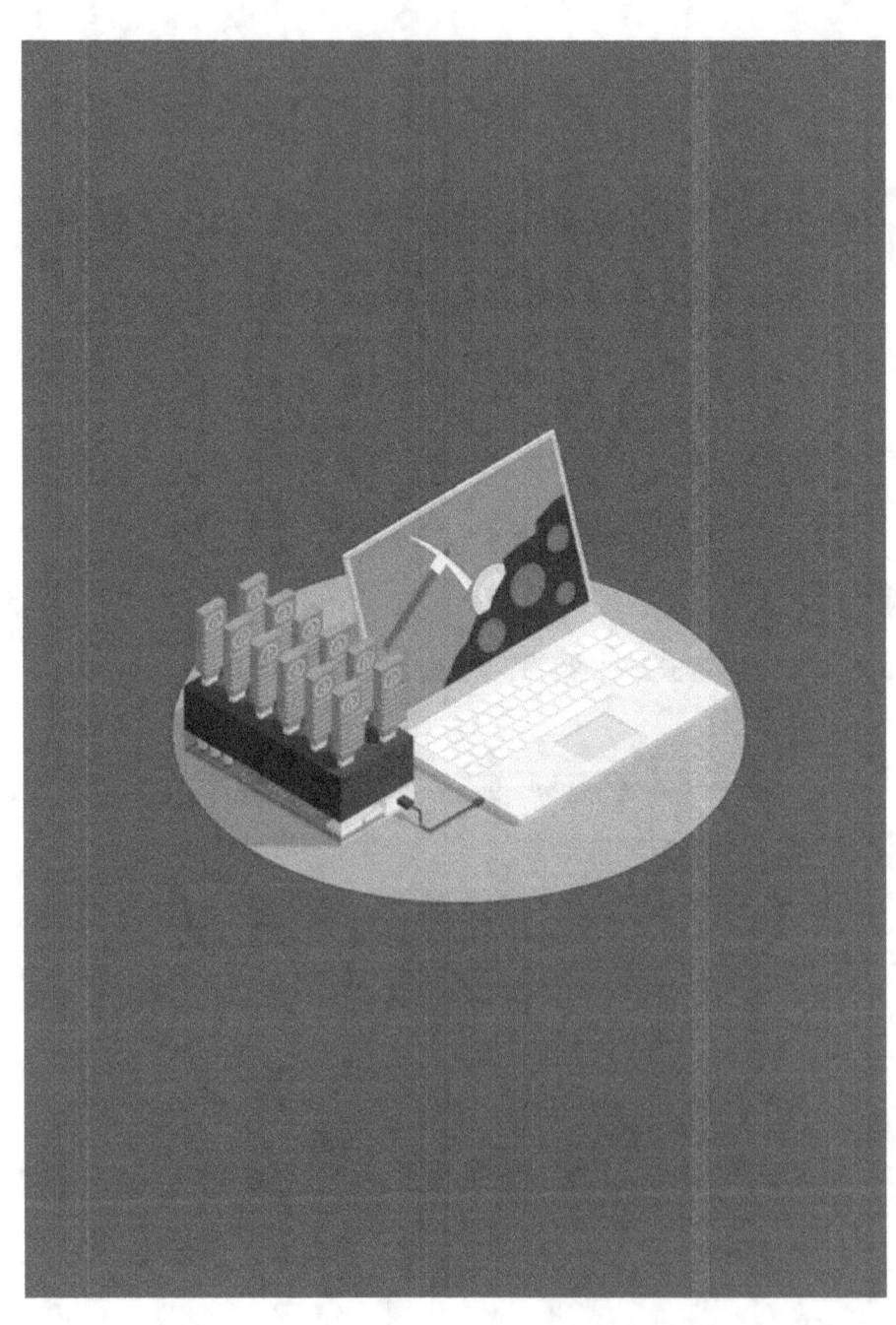

Bonus Chapter: Bitcoin Mining Essentials: The Benefits and how it works

Bitcoins mining helps in generating Bitcoins until the 21 million-limit set on it has been reached. The number of Bitcoins in circulation can be increased by mining and at present only about half of the Bitcoins have been extracted. Unlike conventional currencies, Bitcoins aren't issued by banks, governments, or any other regulatory authorities. Several complex mathematical equations need to be solved for mining Bitcoins.

This process is resource intensive, and the number of people competing for unearthing Bitcoins has increased considerably. As the competition increases, the difficulty level of these equations increases as well. To solve an equation on the blockchain, you will need a good mining rig and a couple of days. Also, a lot of electricity will be required by the computer for solving these equations.

The costs involved don't make it viable as an innocent hobby. A Bitcoin rig requires a substantial investment and electricity. The platform needs to keep running for a couple of days at a time for cracking the code so that you will need an efficient cooling system too. Due to the costs that are involved, miners tend to come together to pool their resources for Bitcoin mining.

In the conventional system of fiat currency, governments all over the world are responsible for printing money. However, Bitcoins cannot be written, and they need to be discovered. Computers and users across the globe compete against one another for mining these Bitcoins. The Bitcoin network can also be made use of for transferring Bitcoins across the world. This system guarantees anonymity unless someone keeps track of who is sending what to whom.

The Bitcoin network makes this possible by collecting all the data about transactions taking place in a given period and compile it all into a list. This list is known as a block. A miner essentially confirms these deals and records them into a ledger. This ledger is made up of different blocks and is collectively known as a blockchain. Each entry in this list can be filed only when a transaction occurs between two Bitcoin addresses. Whenever a new record is created, it will be added to the existing blockchain. That produces a lengthy list of deals. Every miner on the network will be provided with an updated copy of the block so that they are aware of the happenings on the blockchain.

You might be wondering if this ledger can be trusted, primarily when the data is being held in digital form. How can this network be secured so that it isn't tampered with? Well, this is where the miners come in. Whenever a block of transactions is recorded, the miners put it through a specific process. A mathematical equation is applied to the information that is held within a block so that it is transformed into something different. It produces a hash, and it is a short sequence of seemingly random letters and numbers.

A mixture is stored in the block at the end of the blockchain network. These hashes have interesting properties. It is quite easy to create a hash from all the information that's available. However, it isn't easy to determine what the original data that was used to generate the hash was. Each hash is unique, and even if one character in a single hash is altered, there will be a domino effect on the entire blockchain.

The transactions recorded in the blocks help in generating the "hash." Every block on the network consists of the hash of the previous block of the Bitcoin blockchain. It forms a digital seal that cannot be broken without alerting all the miners on the network. It also provides the necessary confirmation regarding the legality of every block on the blockchain network. Even if a small portion of a block has been tampered with, then others will know. If a fraudulent transaction is tried to be included on the network, then this will change the hash of the block within which it is being recorded.

If someone were to check the legitimacy of the

transaction by running it through a hashing equation, the false comparison would stand out like a sore thumb. Since the hash of a block is used for producing the hash of the subsequent block, tampering with one hash will result in an alteration in the following hash as well. It will cause a domino effect that would change the entire network.

The network is as secure as the users who use it. The Bitcoin network is supported by running the nodes or by dedicating the required computational power of the mining rig into the public ledger and the accounting part of the blockchain network. Since this power isn't concentrated in the hands of a few users, it becomes quite difficult to break this chain or even forge new coins. All the computation prowess that's dedicated towards the Bitcoin blockchain reduces its vulnerability of being hacked. The incentive that keeps the miners motivated would be the Bitcoins that they will receive whenever a new block is mined. Mining isn't a simple process, and transactions cannot be duplicated on the network since every operation is verified by multiple miners on the web.

Starting your Bitcoin mine

- It has become slightly tough to start your Bitcoin mine these days when compared to how it was a couple of years ago. The competition in this field has increased manifold. Mining hardware that is used has also evolved quite a bit, and now some computers can be made use of for cracking those mathematical equations easily. It is incredibly important that you have got the right hardware for this job. The equipment you will want to invest in will depend on your budget and your expectation of profit from the rig. People used to make use of PCs and laptops for mining Bitcoins back in 2009.

  During the first few weeks after the launch of Bitcoins, only a few people were interested in mining the Bitcoins that were in existence. Soon the enthusiasts had discovered a way in which they could make use of the graphics card of the computer for cracking the algorithm. The graphics card computes the date, and it renders this in the form of a video game on the computer. With a little bit of tweaking, people had realized that the graphics card could be successfully made use of for mining Bitcoins profitably. When Bitcoins are mined by making use of GPU instead of a CPU, their productivity can be substantially increased. It did not take much time for the CPU, and the GPU system of decoding went obsolete and got replaced by FPGA. An FPGA is a field programmable gate array. What FPGAs changed was that they managed to provide just as much computational power as most GPUs and CPUs of 2013, but consumed a drastically lesser amount of electric power. Soon, Bitcoin ASICs were all the rage, and they performed much better than the GPUs and FPGAs. The consumption of electricity could also be reduced by making use of ASICs, but it does generate a lot of sounds and this can be quite troubling if need to be put up with for prolonged periods of time. Not just the noise, the mining rig that makes use of ASICs can generate a lot of heat as well.

- A couple of things that you should keep in mind before you set up your Bitcoin mining rig. The cost of mining Bitcoins can exceed the investment that you needed for setting up the mining rig. You should also check the local electricity schemes to check whether it would be viable or not. An average miner would need about 12.4kw of energy per hour. By figuring out the cost of electricity, you will be able to ascertain whether the likely income generated from the rig would outweigh the costs that you will have to incur to keep it running. The rig will also need regular maintenance and upkeep. This means the platform will require constant attention as well as a recurring expense incurred for maintenance. This is a recurring cost because the machine is bound to break down after running the code for hours trying to crack it. One important thing that you will have to keep in mind before you set your rig is that apart from financial investment, you will need to invest your time and energy in it as well. Several online websites are available that you can make use of for checking whether it would be profitable to set up your mining rig or not. These applications will do all the necessary calculations and provide you with an answer that will help you in making the decision.

- Bitcoin mining isn't an easy hobby. It will take time, resources, effort, and commitment if you want to take it up seriously. This isn't a child's play, and you will get the hang of it with the passage of time.

- You can always start mining for Bitcoins on your own, or you can even form a group and start mining collectively. Decide the manner in which the proceedings should be distributed and get to work. Bitcoin mining these days requires excellent technical and computing prowess, so starting your Bitcoin mining group is a pretty good idea.

CHAPTER SUMMARY:

- Bitcoin mining is akin to mining for any precious metal. The only difference is that in the case of Bitcoins, the mining is done digitally. The blocks of data on blockchain are mined for producing a hash, and the correct hash will provide the miner with 25 Bitcoins as a reward.

- Bitcoin mining requires dedicated computers and software with high computing power.
- Bitcoin mining can be done in groups or even individually.

YOUR QUICK START ACTION STEP:

In this chapter, you were introduced to the concept of Bitcoin mining. However, before you consider taking up Bitcoin mining, you should acquire more information about the same. You should head over to www.coinstaker.com to learn more about Bitcoin mining.

Conclusion

Thank you again for owning this book!

I hope this book was able to help you to learn more about the fascinating world of Bitcoins.

The next step is to select a Bitcoin exchange that you would want to trade on, select a Bitcoin wallet, and get started with trading Bitcoins. Alternatively, you can take up Bitcoin mining, join a Bitcoin mining group, or even invest in Bitcoin mining. Investing in Bitcoins is a wonderful idea since the popularity of Bitcoins is just increasing and it will not slow down anytime soon. Bitcoins ushered in the age of digitized currencies that can revolutionize the world. So, what are you waiting for? There is no time like the present to jump aboard the Bitcoin bandwagon. The two essential qualities that you should work on if you want to make money with the Bitcoins are patience and a willingness to learn.

Finally, if this book has given you value and helped you in any way, then I'd like to ask you for a favor if you would be kind enough to leave a review for this book on Amazon? It'd be much appreciated!

Thank you and good luck!

About the Author

Gavin S. Finney is a Bitcoin and cryptocurrency investor who has written several books on the subject.

As a successful investor, he then got interested in digital currency and Bitcoin during its early stages, but got frustrated learning the technical topic.

Gavin wanted a method that he could easily learn from in order to understand all about digital currency and how to make money out of it. He soon discovered a teaching series online that made him learn faster and better.

Applying the same approach, Gavin successfully made his first digital currency transaction which triggered the start of his digital currency success.

With the books that he writes on the subject matter, he aims to provide readers with great value and in the hopes that they too can experience the same success investing and making money from cryptocurrency.

www.ingramcontent.com/pod-product-compliance
Lightning Source LLC
Chambersburg PA
CBHW071321220526
45468CB00001B/454